Original title:

Waves of Paradise

Copyright © 2025 Creative Arts Management OÜ

All rights reserved.

Author: Amelia Montgomery

ISBN HARDBACK: 978-1-80581-478-8

ISBN PAPERBACK: 978-1-80581-005-6

ISBN EBOOK: 978-1-80581-478-8

Glittering Horizon

On a beach where seagulls dance,
Sandcastles sprout, not by chance.
A crab in a suit, quite the sight,
Hobbling along, oh what a fright!

Sun hats bob like cheerful boats,
With sunscreen lotion, we'll gloat.
Flip-flops flapping, we sprint, we race,
Chasing ice cream in a sweet embrace.

Under the sun, our worries float,
As laughter bubbles, we stay remote.
A dolphin wears glasses, quite a tease,
While seaweed dances with perfect ease.

Day fades softly, painted skies flare,
We chase fireflies without a care.
In this land, where giggles reside,
We find joy on this humor-filled ride.

The Sun's Lullaby on the Sea

The sun wears sunglasses, oh so bright,
It swings on the horizon, a comical sight.
Seagulls cracking jokes as they flap about,
While fish play it cool, swimming in and out.

The beach ball bounces, takes a quick dive,
Sandy feet race, trying to survive.
A crab with a hat scuttles away,
Chasing a shrimp that dares to sway.

Tidal Serenade

The tide hums tunes as it rolls and swells,
Starfish are dancing, ringing their bells.
Shells gather gossip from the ocean floor,
While clams tell tales that leave us wanting more.

A dolphin flips over, steals the show,
With a splash and a giggle, off it goes.
Seaweed does the cha-cha with flair,
In this ocean party, we all want to share.

Driftwood Dreams

Driftwood's a couch, we lie and lounge,
Imagining pirates that frown and scrounge.
A treasure map drawn on a napkin near,
With chocolate coins, oh, let's have a cheer!

Octopus juggles while we sip lemonade,
A flip of the script, let's start a parade.
Beach hats and flip-flops take center stage,
We laugh till we cry, let's turn the page.

Cradle of Sheltered Bliss

Under the palms, it's a shady retreat,
Where coconuts fall with a soft little beat.
Laughter erupts as one hits the sand,
A surprise party for the unsuspecting hand.

Sunscreen battles, slippery and wild,
Making kids giggle, each parent's lost child.
We build castles that tumble with grace,
As waves come rushing, we giggle and race.

Enchanted Coves of Delight

In hidden nooks where seagulls squawk,
We sip our drinks and laugh a lot.
With sandy toes and silly grins,
We wiggle around like goofy pins.

The crabs throw parties on the shore,
Dancing sideways, who could ask for more?
With beach balls flying everywhere,
We catch the sun without a care.

Resplendent Rays and Ocean Hues

Sunblock slathered on our face,
We prance around at a comical pace.
Fish peek out with curious eyes,
As we plop in and out with surprise.

Shiny shells become our bling,
We strut like queens and kings.
The dolphins giggle, splash, and play,
While we try not to lose our way.

Heartbeats in the Celestial Waters

With splashes loud and voices bright,
We chase the tide by day and night.
But who needs grace? We leap and fall,
Like fish on land, we have a ball.

A pelican drops in for a snack,
We laugh so hard, we lose our track.
With every flop and graceful blunder,
We find pure joy in our wet wonder.

Lullabies of the Tidepool Dream

The seaweed tickles, oh what fun!
Singing songs beneath the sun.
With hermit crabs that steal the show,
We cheer them on as they all go slow.

Starfish giggle on the rocks,
While we joke about our socks.
The tide pools shimmer, dance, and gleam,
As we float on our imagination's beam.

Horizons Beckon the Soul

The horizon grins with glee,
As seagulls dance, so wild and free.
I thought I saw a fish in shoes,
But it was just the ocean's blues.

A crab joined in the conga line,
While starfish sipped on salty brine.
The ocean murmurs jokes and cheer,
A comical scene, oh dear, oh dear!

Journey Through Marine Reverie.

I sailed on dreams, a boat of cheese,
With jellyfish as crew, if you please.
They laughed and jiggled with delight,
A charming sight in the morning light.

An octopus offered me a hat,
Said it was stylish, better than that!
With eight arms waving, how could I say,
"Thanks, but I think I'll pass today"?

Ocean's Embrace

A whale wore sunglasses, cool as ice,
Claiming the sun was quite the slice.
Fish flipping around in bubbles galore,
Chasing their tails, oh what a chore!

A sea turtle offered me some tea,
I sipped it slowly, feeling so free.
But then a dolphin stole my spot,
"I'm taking a break—deal with the knot!"

Celestial Tides

Stars above do a swimming jig,
While the moon plays peek-a-boo, oh big!
The ocean sparkles like a party hat,
Wave your arms, it's time to chat!

A sea cucumber wrote a song,
It was quite catchy, but way too long.
I danced along, though out of tune,
With laughter echoing 'neath the moon.

Harmony in Liquid Motion

Splashing feet on sandy shores,
Seagulls squawk, but who keeps scores?
A crab did dance, oh what a sight,
With sideways moves, it stole the night.

Flipping over, the fish take flight,
While turtles bask in soft moonlight.
With every swirl and playful cheer,
The ocean's giggle brings us near.

Light's Journey Across the Blue

Sunbeams prance, a gleeful race,
Chasing shadows with a smiling face.
Mermaids laugh, sipping on pink foam,
While starfish draw their maps of home.

The dolphins do a belly flop,
While jellybeans go hop, hop, hop.
Under a sky of candy floss,
The ocean's here to show who's boss.

Beneath the Ocean's Lullaby

Coral castles made of dreams,
Fish in tuxedos, or so it seems.
The octopus knits with a sly grin,
Eavesdrops on gossip from a fin.

Turtles snore in a seaweed bed,
While clams gossip, wide-eyed and red.
Bubbles pop like jokes on a spree,
Who knew the deep could be so free?

Rhythms of Maritime Melodies

A ukulele played by a whale,
Seagulls hum, with a fishy tale.
The sea cucumbers tap their toes,
While crabs breakdance and steal the shows.

Dancing ripples sway in time,
Anemones sway to the beat and chime.
Every splash tells a story untold,
In water's arms, life's joys unfold.

The Mirage of Seabreeze

A crab in shades, sipping soda,
Claims the beach is his pagoda.
Seagulls laugh at his grand tales,
While chasing after fishy wails.

Flip-flops dance on sandy floors,
As sunburned tourists hunt for stores.
One lost hat takes flight and spins,
A seagull snatches, laughing grins!

Inflatable flamingo floats by,
As mermaids wave and wink an eye.
Someone's cat just caught a tan,
Who needs a boat? Just bring a fan!

At sunset's glow, the laughter rings,
With all of nature's silly things.
This mirage of fun, we can't resist,
Life's a beach that we've all missed!

Echoing Infinity

An echo calls, 'Come here and play!'
But it's just a parrot, hip hooray!
Who knows what secrets it may keep,
In its beak, our giggles leap!

The ocean fights with every splash,
While dolphins bounce and have a clash.
They tell the stars to mind their space,
As moonbeams join the silly race!

Merriment erupts from every foam,
With imaginary friends, we roam.
A beachball bounces to the sky,
Is that a whale or just a pie?

Beneath the sun, we wiggle, twirl,
As laughter dances, hearts unfurl.
In this infinity, fun won't cease,
Each echo whispers blissful peace!

Wanderlust in Blue

With every step, a splash so bright,
In a puddle, shoes take flight.
A curious octopus winks and sways,
As flip-flops squeak in summer's rays!

Sandcastles rise but meet their fate,
As waves tiptoe, it's quite the date.
Shells giggle as they hide and seek,
A golden crab will sneak a peek!

Mermaids grin with starfish in tow,
In snorkels upside-down, off we go.
But the tide tricks us all to fall,
Making water's surface a free-for-all!

In this blue, our hearts do soar,
With laughter bubbling on the shore.
Wanderlust, it knows no pause,
In this silly life, we just applaud!

Embrace of the Horizon's Touch

The sun dips low, a painted trend,
While clumsy pelicans descend.
They miss their mark, a splashy flop,
Belly flops from sky to crop!

Footprints lead to hidden treasure,
A sandwich lost, what a displeasure!
Seashells gossip, 'What's that smell?'
But giggles rise, it's all quite swell!

The surf sings songs of quirky fish,
Each one dreams of a wild dish.
As tide pools boast their slimy charms,
And wink at crabs with fuzzy arms!

In these moments, time holds still,
As laughter flows, a joyful thrill.
In the embrace of day's warm clutch,
We cherish life's bright, silly touch!

Celestial Drift

Floating on the clouds, oh what a sight,
Rubber ducks racing, all through the night.
With popcorn in hand, we cheer and we shout,
As jellybeans swim, there's no hint of doubt.

Seagulls in tutus dance with delight,
While octopuses play cards, what a night!
Bubbles of laughter burst like balloons,
In this carnival, we dance to the tunes.

The Ocean's Sweet Caress

Seashells laughing at the shore's funny joke,
As fish throw a party, that's no hoax.
Crabs wearing sunglasses strut down the sand,
With a cocktail in claws, it's all so grand.

Nudging tides tickle toes with their tease,
While starfish gossip about the breeze.
Jellyfish giggle, doing the flip,
In a splashy parade, not one is a trip.

Currents of Elysian Whispers

Mermaids are sleeping, don't wake them, please,
As dolphins are plotting a sneak to tease.
Waves break in laughter, crash like a snort,
While sea turtles plan their hilarious sport.

Sandcastles wobble, then fall in a heap,
As seasocks appear, from their sandy sleep.
Anemones wiggle with a cheeky grin,
When crabs tell tall tales, and all join in.

Liquid Continuum

Fish in tuxedos swim to the beat,
Sardines forming conga lines, what a feat!
An underwater circus, with humor galore,
As bubbles fly up, laughter starts to soar.

With a splash and a giggle, the whales sing loud,
Comedic performers, they draw a big crowd.
Sea cucumbers schmooze in their slick little dance,
Each fin and each flipper—who took that chance?

Tranquil Reflections

In a hammock strung from dreams,
A fish wears my sunglasses.
Seagulls throw shade like pros,
While I snooze and take a pass.

The sun's a hot potato,
Baking my curly hair.
Crabs gather for a disco,
Dancing like they just don't care.

A dolphin steals my sandwich,
I chase it with a shrug.
It winks, and off it zips,
Leaving me with just a mug.

As twilight paints a canvas,
Jellybeans drop from the sky.
I grab a handful for dinner,
A tasty snack, oh my!

Beneath the Starlit Sea

The stars hold secrets, it seems,
Mermaids giggle in the dark.
Octopuses serenade dreams,
While sea turtles share a lark.

Bubbles pop like champagne corks,
Fish sporting monocles prance.
Starfish spin in silly shorts,
Joining in the dance of chance.

Jellyfish float like balloons,
In wild and glowy attire.
Shells whisper jokes to the moon,
As crabs jam out by the fire.

The ocean's a punchline, oh yes,
A chuckle wrapped in foam.
With a flick of my tail, I confess,
I'm a star in this aquatic dome!

Portals to Bliss

A sandcastle full of dreams,
With windows and a moat.
Seagulls swoop down for ice creams,
Caught in a tasty boat.

Flip-flops dance on sandy feet,
As sunburned toes turn red.
Clams with hats feel quite the heat,
As ocean blues paint the spread.

Laughter bubbles like the foam,
I share a joke with a seal.
Mermaids swim by with a comb,
Claiming I'm their big deal.

In this land of pure delight,
Where giggles float on air.
I'll ride the waves of happy light,
With jellybeans everywhere!

Celestial Foam

The sun's a slice of pizza,
Melting into the sea.
Lobsters wear party hats,
And dance in jubilee.

Bubbles burst into laughter,
As fish tell jokes galore.
Starfish flash their best bling,
While crabs break out the floor.

The ocean's a cosmic stage,
Where laughter fills the skies.
Mermaids twirl with glee and rage,
While sea cucumbers sigh.

So grab a wave of chuckles,
And ride it 'til you're done.
Let the universe be tickled,
As we bask in this fun!

Serenity's Horizon

On a beach where seagulls play,
The sun makes everything okay.
A crab in shades, so very cool,
Is ruling this sandy school.

The tides are laughing at my hat,
It's now a boat for a fuzzy rat.
I chase my shoes as they take flight,
And watch the fish giggle in delight.

Sandy toes and sunscreen's might,
A jellyfish just said 'goodnight.'
I slip on shells, a slip 'n' slide,
With laughter echoing at my side.

Echoes of the Coral Garden

In a reef where colors clash,
A fish with glasses makes a splash.
He winked at me, a cheeky grin,
As I spilled my snack, oh what a sin!

A sea turtle busts a funky move,
While starfish try to find their groove.
Corals chuckle, oh so bright,
Who needs disco when you've got light?

Anemones wave with flair and style,
A clownfish jokes, "Stay for a while!"
They tease the shrimp for being shy,
Dancing 'round like they can fly.

Dance of the Gentle Surf

The ocean's pulse is a friendly beat,
With silly rocks that trip your feet.
A dolphin's flip—a splashy show,
He stole my drink, the little rogue!

I tried to surf, but oh, what grace?
Ended up with sand on my face.
The seals are laughing, it's so clear,
They sip cocktails and cheer my fear!

A surfboard gives advice, I swear,
"Just ride the breeze without a care!"
But I'm tanking faster than a star,
Maybe I'll stick to the beach bar.

Ethereal Shores

On shores where dreams and giggles meet,
A clam shells out jokes, oh what a feat!
I join in on sandy debates,
While sea urchins act like states.

The crabs are chefs, flipping fries,
With sea lettuce, oh what a surprise!
They serve up laughs on a silver plate,
While fishy friends all celebrate.

A netted outfit I did wear,
Caught a crab, who doesn't care.
He looked at me, gave a grumpy stare,
And shuffled off, beyond all flair.

Secrets Beneath the Azure

In deep blue, fish wear ties,
They gossip under sunny skies.
Starfish tease, with silly grins,
As octopuses play violin fins.

Crabs dance silly on the sand,
With beach balls flying hand in hand.
Seashells laugh, what a delight,
Eels twirl round, 'Oh what a sight!'

Gulls debate, who's the best diver,
While dolphins honk like a horned driver.
Flounders dodge with fishy flair,
While turtles race, but go nowhere.

So when you're near the ocean wide,
Join in the fun, let laughter glide.
With every splash and silly tale,
Nature's laughter will prevail!

Cascade of Dreams

Bubbles rise like giggles spun,
In the sea, all laughs are fun.
Jellyfish tickle, they float around,
While seahorses dance to the sound.

Starry nights, fish wear masks,
Doing crazy, underwater tasks.
Mermaids giggle, there's no doubt,
They prank the dolphins when they shout.

Sandy tumbleweeds roll with glee,
As crabs play cards with a cup of tea.
Seashells sing off-key, what a tune,
As surfboards race where the sun's a boon.

Join the giggles, loose your cares,
Where dreams tumble down the stairs.
In this splashy, silly scene,
Life's a joke, bright and serene!

Luminous Waters

Glowing fish in disco lights,
Dance all night in funky flights.
Crabs with shades and jiving hips,
Throwing parties on their trips.

Neon seaweed sways with ease,
As dolphins surf the tiny breeze.
Turtles wear their party hats,
Down under, it's a world of chats.

Bubble parties, drinks in hand,
Jellybeans rain from a candy land.
Fish in tuxedos float with flair,
Making waves without a care.

Underwater, it's all a game,
Laughing at the silly fame.
Luminous dreams, a joyous twist,
In this party, you can't resist!

Sunkissed Shores

On sandy beaches, laughter erupts,
Seagulls dive, all dressed in cups.
Flip-flops waddle, they jog so slow,
While sunbathers boast about their glow.

Sandcastle kings with paper crowns,
Defend their lands from laughing clowns.
With shells as trumpets, songs they play,
As crabs march in a grand ballet.

Beach balls fly, a game ensues,
While everyone searches for lost blue shoes.
Kites high above, they swirl and sway,
On sunkissed shores, it's a silly day.

Families frolic, dogs chase the tide,
Rolling in sand with joy and pride.
Beach life's funny, oh what a show,
In the sun's embrace, let the laughter flow!

Horizon's Embrace

A fish in a tux, what a sight!
He dances and twirls, oh what a delight.
With jellyfish friends in their best shades,
They party 'til dawn with crab parades.

Seagulls attempt to steal their snack,
But the fish just laugh, "We won't hold back!"
With flips and flops, they dodge their fate,
In this ocean dance, they celebrate fate.

Harmony of the Ocean's Breath

A clam with a comb, feeling quite neat,
Sings a tune that's offbeat, oh so sweet.
Octopus on drums, he keeps the time,
With a tune so absurd, it's a silly rhyme.

Starfish join in with a clumsy twist,
They dance on the sand, can you resist?
While turtles giggle and join the queue,
In the harmony, they find something new.

Glimmers of Ocean Light

A flounder named Fred wears a shiny crown,
He thinks he's the king of this colorful town.
With bubbles of laughter, they light up the bay,
And they prank all the sharks, oh what a display!

Dolphins in shades surf the sun's golden rays,
While the seaweed wiggles in merry ballet.
They tackle the tides in a goofy parade,
In the glow of the sea, their shenanigans played.

Rhapsody of the Silent Cove

In a cove where the crabs like to chat,
They gossip and giggle, oh how they spat.
With shells used as hats, they strut with pride,
This quirky brigade shows no need to hide.

A whale tells a joke, and the sea cows are shy,
As the barnacles chuckle, they nearly cry.
In this silent cranny, hilarity flows,
With friendship and laughter, the fun always grows.

Glimmers of Aquatic Dreams

Under the sea where fish wear hats,
A dolphin laughs, and who knows that?
Turtles doing yoga, a real dance show,
While jellybeans float in a grand row.

Crabs hold a party, pinch and tease,
While seahorses try to catch a breeze.
The seaweed sways with a boisterous beat,
As sea cucumbers shuffle to their own seat.

Starfish giggle at a fish's joke,
An octopus dons a monocle cloak.
With bubbles of laughter and joy galore,
The ocean's antics are never a bore.

Corals compete in a colorful race,
Waving their arms in a funny embrace.
In this watery world where wonders gleam,
Life is a splash, in an aquatic dream.

Twilight Caress of Distant Shores

At dusk, the crabs gather for a chat,
While seagulls plot to steal a fish mat.
Oysters play cards, no one keeps score,
And clams are just waiting to tell you more.

The lighthouse winks with glimmers bright,
As waves whisper secrets, oh what a sight!
A surfer stumbles, makes quite the scene,
Splashing around like a well-dressed bean.

A boat full of fish, all dressed in flair,
Dreaming of land, oh, is it really fair?
With barnacles dancing, they break out in song,
Life's little oddities always belong.

The twilight paints everything with glee,
As starfish practice their best belly.
Tonight let's play, in humor we thrive,
Under the shimmer, we come alive!

Serenity Beneath the Sun-Kissed Waves

Beneath the sun, the fish flip and flop,
As crabs perform their clumsy hop.
Seashells gossip, spilling the tea,
On who's the prettiest under the sea.

A starfish lounges, soaking the rays,
While plankton dance in an ocean ballet.
A whale sings off-key, trying to charm,
But all his notes just raise the alarm.

Sand dollars create a relaxed vibe,
They throw a fiesta, what a jive!
Starry-eyed fish wear their best bling,
While shrimp start a conga, it's quite the fling.

Under the surface, life's laughter swells,
With tales and giggles in seaweed's bells.
A carnival of jellyfish flitting about,
In this sun-kissed realm, there's never a doubt.

Crystalline Dreams of the Deep

In the deep blue, where the giggles reside,
Fish play hide and seek, they're tough to guide.
Anemones tickle, it feels quite strange,
While squids compete for the weirdest range.

Bright coral castles hold a grand ball,
Where seaweed twirls, and the clams enthrall.
Octopuses juggle, not a single slip,
While snails breakdance, oh what a trip!

Anglerfish beam with their glowing lights,
As clownfish quip on wrong turns in fights.
Bubbles rise high, carrying tales galore,
In this underwater world, laughter's the core.

Crystalline dreams play tricks on your brain,
As friendly fish dance in the shimmering rain.
Let the current drift you to funny delight,
In this quirky kingdom, everything's right.

Chasing the Horizon's Embrace

In a boat made of chips and dreams,
I sailed on a soda stream.
The gulls above threw popcorn down,
While I paddled with a flip-flop crown.

The sun got jealous of my tan,
As I tried to catch a bouncing can.
With sunscreen smeared from ear to ear,
I danced with crabs and drank some beer.

But the seagulls plotted their advance,
They swooped for snacks as I tried to prance.
They squawked and shrieked with such delight,
While I just wished for a push-up fight.

As the tides would giggle and spit,
I pondered whether I'd ever fit.
But with every splosh and silly splash,
I learned that life's just a joyful bash.

Whispers of Salty Zephyrs

The breeze tickled my nose just right,
As I tried to hold my sandwich tight.
It danced away, oh what a trick,
A game of chase, the wind quite slick!

With seagulls joining in my plight,
They stole my fries; it gave me fright!
I threw a chip, they took the bait,
And all I got was food on my plate.

The sun was laughing, I was too,
With my hat flying, what could I do?
I chased my hat across the sand,
While the ocean giggled, oh so grand.

A crab waved hello with a pinch so sly,
I danced away while letting out a cry.
But in this madness, all I found,
Were whispers sweet where joy is found.

Mirage of the Distant Isles

I thought I spied some treasure chests,
But it was just some old sun-drenched vests.
I laughed so hard I lost my shade,
As my dreams of riches slowly fade.

The hammock turned into a swinging beast,
As I tumbled over, to say the least.
With coconuts rolling through my hair,
I swore I'd find a comfy chair!

Then a crab snuck in for a taste of fun,
Tried to steal the sun and run.
I chased it down, my flip-flops flew,
While people laughed, oh, what a view!

But dusk arrived with a glittering sway,
And brought to end my silly play.
I left the beach with rocks and sand,
And dreams of mirages still so grand.

The Rhythm of the Endless Blue

With a ukulele, I sang out loud,
While whales below formed a dancing crowd.
Their bubbles burst like notes in song,
I couldn't help but sing along!

The dolphins flipped, I clapped my hands,
They wore sunglasses, making plans.
The ocean floor had its own parade,
Of fish in costumes, brightly displayed.

But a jellyfish thought it was a ballet,
As I stepped right and it danced away.
I twirled around, what a silly sight,
While barnacles cheered under the moonlight.

So I strummed a tune on my sandy stage,
And let the tide be my turning page.
With laughter echoing far and wide,
I knew in this bliss, I'd forever glide.

Reflections in the Crystal Sea

In the shimmering light, fish wear hats,
Jellybeans swim with silly spats.
Seagulls gossip with a cheeky glance,
While dolphins decide to throw a dance.

Turtles race with teeth so bright,
One tripped over a seashell, what a sight!
The seaweed wiggles, joins the fun,
As crabs compete in a sprint, just for a run.

The sun sneezes, oh what a scare,
Splashing laughter fills the salty air.
Shells giggle softly as they spin,
Treasures waiting for a wily grin.

In the crystal sea, laughter flows,
Every creature puts on a show.
With flips and flops, they all agree,
Life is better in a fishy spree!

Tranquil Echoes of the Horizon

Mermaids munch on popcorn by noon,
They invite the seagulls to join a tune.
The horizon winks with a playful beam,
While crabs break out in a funky dream.

Clouds like cotton candy float on by,
Stars hiding out, too shy to try.
The ocean giggles, bubbles in delight,
As octopuses juggle under the moonlight.

Sunsets wear tutus, twirl with flair,
Shells compete who can dance in the air.
Salty dogs bark out a merry bark,
As fishes ride scooters—what a lark!

At the horizon's edge, joy does reign,
As laughter echoes in the sea's refrain.
In whimsical bliss, we all agree,
No place like this for shenanigans and glee!

The Lure of Celestial Shores

On emergent sands, the starfish play,
Making sandcastles that brighten the day.
Crabs wear sunglasses, looking quite fine,
While seagulls strut in a line, divine.

Tides tickle toes with a gentle tease,
As shrimp wear bow ties in the evening breeze.
Dolphins tell jokes, and the fish all cheer,
With each wave that crashes, more laughter near.

Anemones host a fancy ball,
With plankton dancing, answer their call.
Sand dollars sing a nostalgic tune,
Beneath the warm glow of a silvery moon.

At celestial shores, life's a big play,
Comedy thrives in every wave's sway.
Join the fiesta, don't be a bore,
In this funny realm, you'll always want more!

Secrets of the Sunlit Cove

In the cove where secrets are shared,
Starfish scribble notes, feeling prepared.
Shrimp give high fives, their tails in the air,
While clams hold meetings—just don't be square.

Sea turtles hide treasures, a burger or two,
Clams squeal with laughter at what's in the stew.
Golden rays tickle the surface so bright,
In this cove of wonders, all feels just right.

Coral reefs are the best stage of all,
Fish start a dance-off—who will take the fall?
The water's a splash fest, colors abound,
In the sunlit cove, mirth knows no bounds.

Every secret spills, all creatures unite,
Under the sun, joy takes endless flight.
From turtles to otters, come out for fun,
At the cove, life's a party—never a run!

Embrace of the Coral Caress

Bubbles dance, a fishy show,
Bright palates paint the ebb and flow.
Octopus plays peek-a-boo with glee,
While seahorses waltz like it's a spree.

A crab in a tux, oh what a sight,
Crawls out for dinner, oh what a fright!
With clams in the chorus, singing so loud,
It's an undersea bash; it's quite the crowd!

The starfish spins tales, it's quite a feat,
While the sea urchins can't find their seat.
Jellyfish giggle, they float with flair,
Swaying and swirling in salty air.

So let's dive deep; it's a bubbly place,
Where critters and laughter set the pace.
Join in the fun and splash away,
In this coral embrace, dance through the spray!

Harmonies of the Gentle Surf

The pelicans sing, a clumsy tune,
Chasing the waves beneath a laughing moon.
Surfboards tumble; it's comic relief,
As surfers perform their own brand of grief.

Seagulls squawk with a snazzy beat,
While crabs in sunglasses just can't be beat.
An otter's on a float, sipping some tea,
Says, 'This ocean life is so full of glee!'

Fish flip-flop with a splashy grin,
Each dive and swirl pulls you right in.
Turtles race while dodging a wave,
Like a slow-motion match to be brave.

But when the tide giggles and plays,
You can't help but join in their crazy ways.
The sound of joy will never fade,
In this surf harmony, a new world made!

Unfurling Petals of the Sea

Corals bloom like flowers aglow,
In colors that dance, a vibrant show.
A dolphin prances, quite a clown,
In this undersea garden, where joys abound.

Anemones wave, putting on a cheer,
Wiggly and wobbly, so brightly near.
A pufferfish pops, it's a comical sight,
While clownfish laugh at their awkward flight.

Starfish serenade the folks on the shore,
With seaweed swaying, oh, they want more.
The ocean smiles wide, with giggles to share,
In this floral fiesta, joy fills the air.

So dip your toes in the silly stream,
Where bubbles and laughter make the world beam.
Embrace the petals that the sea unveils,
In each frolicsome moment, the joy never fails!

A Tidal Retreat to Serenity

The tide rolls in with giggles and sighs,
A pelican marries a sea gull in disguise.
Seashells gather, gossip and chatter,
As the underwater world starts to matter.

A fish dressed as a pirate leaps high,
While little shrimp share secrets and sigh.
Sandcastles crumble under laughter's weight,
As kids build kingdoms, sealing their fate.

The tide comes back with a playful push,
Rolling in whispers of a giggling hush.
A sea turtle races, no time to retreat,
Chasing its dreams on webbed little feet.

So find your calm amid the fun,
Where laughter mingles with the setting sun.
Splashing in joy, each moment's divine,
In this tidal retreat, we merrily shine!

Depths of Tranquility

In the blue where dolphins dance,
They wiggle and they prance.
Seagulls squawk a silly tune,
While crabs hide beneath the moon.

Fish wear hats, it's quite a sight,
With starfish lounging in the light.
The octopus plays peek-a-boo,
While turtles join the ocean crew.

Jellyfish float with graceful flair,
As seaweed sports a flowing hair.
The corals giggle in bright hues,
A colorful underwater muse.

Here in blissful, wavy lands,
The ocean laughs and sings in bands.
Grab your goggles, take a dive,
In the depths where jests arrive!

Spirit of the Coastal Breeze

The breeze brings tales of fishy pranks,
As surfers throw their funny ranks.
Kites fly high, a playful chase,
While crabs compete in their own race.

Sandcastles topple with a laugh,
As kids discover the ocean's path.
Seashells grin, they're quite the crew,
Hiding secrets, shiny and new.

Beach balls bounce and seagulls tease,
While everyone winds down with ease.
The sun dips low, it's time to play,
As twilight dances, bright and gay.

Laughter echoes, here and there,
In the salty billionaire air.
Embrace the fun, so light and free,
In the spirit of the breeze, you'll see!

Serenity's Secret Cove

Hidden deep where mermaids dwell,
They weave their tales, oh what a spell!
The sea otters hold a tea,
With crumpets served, it's quite the spree.

Clams play cards by the moonlit hush,
While dolphins join in the silly rush.
Starfish gossip in colors bright,
As the night bids the sun goodnight.

Secrets dance in the ocean's lap,
With laughter trapped in nature's wrap.
In this cove, all worries cease,
Where every moment shouts, "Release!"

Oh what joy in the sandy bed,
Nature's antics, laughter spread.
So come again, you'll feel alive,
In this cove, where giggles thrive!

Sway of the Morning Tide

Morning breaks with a ticklish start,
As seashells hum and dolphins dart.
The crabs perform their early jig,
While seagulls argue, loud and big.

A flip-flop hops on lazy sand,
Tales of treasures sift through the hand.
The sunbeams tickle in playful zest,
While the tides announce their morning quest.

Coffee brewed by sandy toes,
As waves whisper secrets nobody knows.
Laughter spills like water clear,
In a tidal dance, the fun draws near.

A just awake and bubbly scene,
As ocean's humor starts to glean.
So join the morning, laugh, and glide,
In the rhythm of the morning tide!

Ephemeral Mystique

The sand tickles toes, oh what a tease,
Seagulls squawk gossip, sharing the breeze.
Flip-flops are flying, a mischievous dance,
As sunscreen gets slapped on by chance.

The tide sneezes bubbles, splashes galore,
Beachballs take flight, who knows where they soar?
A crab with a swagger, calls out 'Hey there!'
While sunburned tourists try not to stare.

Living in moments, we laugh and we cheer,
Each grain is a joke, each splash brings a tear.
Forget your woes, sit back, take a seat,
Life's a swim party—how can it be beat?

With laughter and sun, our spirits take flight,
Counting the gulls till the end of the night.
A toast to the foolish, the silly, the free,
For paradise lives in small acts—just like me!

Seraphic Currents

In breezy attire, we waltz with the tide,
Bikini-clad warriors, with chips on the side.
Surfboards like chariots, galloping fast,
Sunhats protecting the fun from the blast.

Salty air fills our nostrils, we're ready for fun,
Snacking on snacks til the day is all done.
A sandcastle contest? Let's see who's the best,
Oh wait, it collapsed! What a funny jest!

Knock-knock jokes traded 'neath umbrellas aglow,
Igloos made from coolers, where we all will go.
Shells whisper secrets of mermaids and dreams,
While ice cream dribbles like spilled silly creams.

Time slips on by like a fish in the sea,
We're lost in the laughter, just happy and free.
So join in the giggles and let loose your hair,
For every tide's humor is ours to declare!

Oasis Among the Tides

A cooler of laughter, we gather in shade,
With umbrellas for hats, a hilarious parade.
Flip-flops in hand, we march to the shore,
Stomping on crabs, oh what a galore!

Beach chairs in chaos, all tangled with glee,
Kids running wild, while adults sip their tea.
The sun's overhead like a bully on break,
While seagulls steal sandwiches—what a mistake!

Splashing and crashing in puddles of mirth,
Dancing like seaweed, a soft ocean's berth.
The jellyfish giggle as we swim and play,
Chasing each chuckle, the best kind of day!

With sunburned noses and salty sweet grace,
We're the silly ducks in this blissful space.
Life's a bright joke for the brave and the bold,
Let's laugh in the tides as the stories unfold!

Enchanted Beach

The sun waves a wand, making shadows pretend,
Flip-flops are lost, where could they descend?
Sandcastles flourish with moats all around,
While a wayward beach ball takes off with a sound.

Smile at the octopus wearing a cap,
Complaints about sunscreen, just taking a nap.
A dolphin flips, and the crowd breaks in cheer,
'Did you see that move? It's the best of the year!'

Picnics on towels, the spread looks divine,
Except for the ants who just joined for the wine.
Laughter erupts like the tide on the shore,
In this comedy show, who could ask for more?

So here's to the driftwood, the shells, and the fun,
May our laughter linger long after we run.
With treasures we find, let's share every delight,
For life's a loud carnival when summer is bright!

A Symphony of Ocean Breezes

The seagulls squawk in concert's tune,
As beach balls bounce beneath the moon.
A surfer's stunt turns into a flop,
And sandcastles lean, but none dare drop.

The tides play tag with flip-flops lost,
While sunscreen fail draws hilarious cost.
Laughter dances with the salty air,
As sunburnt noses become a rare fare.

Kites take flight in playful chase,
While jellyfish lounge in their odd place.
With sandy sandwiches, a picnic unfolds,
Where laughter is worth more than gold.

So grab your towel and join the fun,
In the silly games where we all run.
For joy is found in this beachy bliss,
In the whimsical ocean, you can't miss!

Celestial Shores of Tranquility

Under the stars, the crabs do dance,
In tiny top hats, they take their chance.
A moonlit tide swirls around their feet,
As they cha-cha while others just tweet.

The clumsy otter steals our snacks,
His antics make us laugh, just relax.
With beach umbrellas tipping in the breeze,
We chuckle as we try to appease.

Sand castling contests go awry,
With towers tumbling, oh my, oh my!
The competition grows quite fierce,
As water balloons grow ever so pierce.

A dolphin flips, what a sight to see,
But loses his lunch, now that's comedy!
Under celestial skies, so vast and bright,
We find our joy in the silly at night.

Beneath the Sapphire Sky

Beneath the azure, skies are aglow,
A sand crab sneaks in, steals the show.
With tiny sunglasses and swagger so grand,
He struts along like he owns the sand.

A pelican drops in for a snack,
Misses the fish - oh, what a whack!
The children giggle, their laughter like song,
As they watch nature's foolishness all day long.

In buckets we build, our dreams take flight,
But seaweed monsters cause quite a fright.
We declare war with plastic spades,
As sandy defenses collapse in cascades.

The sun dips low; it's time to unwind,
With ice cream cones of every kind.
So sit back and roll in the sand, my friend,
For silly moments never truly end.

Dance of the Moonlit Waters

As the moon hangs low, it winks at me,
I try to dance but trip on a seaweed spree.
Salty laughter fills the night air,
With shores aglow, it's a joyous affair.

The starfish gleam with a twinkling gaze,
Their silent applause sets the night ablaze.
While crabs swing by in a conga line,
We join the party with drinks divine.

A beach ball collides with a wayward kite,
While dolphins flip with all their might.
And yet, to my horror, I find it's true,
A seagull snatches my sandwich too!

So let's cheer to nights of unforgettable glee,
In this silly ocean, I escape with glee.
For here under stars, we laugh, and we play,
In the dance of the tide, let merriment stay!

A Symphony of Salt and Dreams

Seagulls squawking like a band,
They steal my lunch, isn't it grand?
The sun is hot, I'm starting to fry,
But the ice cream truck rolls by on the sly.

Buckets and shovels in a heap,
Building castles, but they just droop.
Sand in my toes, all day in the sun,
Oh, the joys of beachside fun!

Splashing around, I trip on a star,
Fell into the drink, now I'm bizarre.
Fish are laughing, what a sight,
At least I'm not out of mind tonight!

Finding treasures, a flip-flop or two,
Laughing at crabs dancing like they're on cue.
With each splash, a giggle escapes,
Welcome to my paradise of capes!

Prism of the Ocean

In the ocean, colors collide,
A fish with polka dots, what a ride!
Sandy chins and sunburned backs,
Giggling children with ice cream snacks.

Dolphins twist in a playful spin,
Seagulls make faces, where do I begin?
The water's chilly, but who really cares?
With every splash, we banish our cares.

Life jackets bobbing, the swim's out of sync,
Uncles in belly flops, making a stink.
But laughter rings out, loud as a bell,
For every slip, there's a story to tell.

As shadows stretch and the day fades away,
We dance in the glow of the golden bay.
Holding our sides in hysterical fits,
Letting the ocean embrace our silly skits.

Glow of the Serene Deep

The beach at dusk is quite a sight,
Flip-flops dangling, what a delight!
Light up the sky with a fizzy drink,
Everyone laughing, with time to blink.

Handstands in sand, falling with grace,
Staring at crabs with a puzzled face.
Why do they scuttle? What's the big rush?
While we're here, let's all just hush.

The ocean whispers secrets to the night,
Mermaids giggle, what a funny plight!
Jellyfish glow like stars in the brine,
As we chase our shadows, feeling divine.

From beach bonfires and ghost stories told,
To the unexpected shivers of cold.
We all know where silly fun keeps,
In the glow of the serene, where laughter leaps.

A Dance with the Nautical Spirits

Under the moon, we find our feet,
Crabs join in, moving to the beat.
Images twirl in the water's embrace,
While I cha-cha far from my place.

Shells and giggles scatter on the sand,
"Are those mermaids?"—no, just my handstand!
The tide rolls in with a mischievous grin,
Washing my cares and chaos within.

Funny old seagulls steal the view,
"Dinner is served!" they squawk loudly too.
The ocean laughs with a watery kiss,
As each splash reminds us of our bliss.

Waltzing with seaweed, what a great scene,
Every misstep caught on the screen.
In the dance of the spirits, the humor is clear,
We twirl in the moonlight, feeling no fear.

Transcendent Waters

The ocean giggles with frothy glee,
As fish wear hats and sip their tea.
Crabs dance a jig, twirling with flair,
Seagulls applaud from the salty air.

Mermaids chuckle, their tails in a twist,
While dolphins perform, none can resist.
Octopuses juggle with slippery grace,
All in this splashy, ridiculous place.

A surfboard sandwich sails on by,
With turtles surfing, oh me, oh my!
The sun throws a party with rays so bright,
While sea cucumbers boogie all night.

When the tide pulls back with a playful fling,
Shells breakdance, and the coral sings.
In these transcendent depths of fun,
The ocean's humor has only begun.

Eternal Embrace of the Sea

In a shell phone call, crabs gossip away,
About fishy fashion and the dolphin ballet.
Starfish dressed sharply in suits made of sand,
Chat about the week with a grand ocean band.

The seaweed sways, it's a dance-off supreme,
As jellyfish glide like a gooey dream.
With sea urchins rolling in laughter and cheer,
Who knew life's a beach? It's crystal clear!

With buckets and shovels, the sharks join the fun,
Digging the ocean; they've just begun.
Their toothy grins sparkle, oh what a sight,
In this eternal embrace, there's pure delight.

Barnacles sing in a humorous tone,
To snappy sea shanties they call their own.
The tide gives a wink, the sun starts to gleam,
In this underwater scene, we happily beam.

Tidal Moonlight

The moon drops in with a mischievous grin,
Tinkling the stars to let laughter begin.
Crabs play charades on the shore's sandy lane,
While fish flash their scales, it's a nighttime soiree!

Glowing soft jellyfish light up the night,
Twisting and turning in phosphorescent flight.
A sea turtle's hat flies off with a snap,
As he chases it down through a seaweed flap.

Seashells are whispering secrets of old,
While the dolphins share tales, oh so bold.
With every splash, the ocean gives cheer,
In tidal moonlight, we banish all fear.

With laughter and joy, the sea starts to play,
As the night dances on, keeping dullness at bay.
In the glow, we waddle, we wiggle, we sway,
Tidal moonlight's embrace makes us want to stay.

Reflections in the Tranquil Swell

Mirrors in water, fish strut and preen,
As they check their looks in this glistening sheen.
Clams offer compliments, all dressed up fine,
While otters trade jokes over a splash of brine.

The sea sings a tune, so merry and bright,
As seagulls join in, taking off in flight.
With laughter and bubbles, the seafoam's a show,
A raucous ensemble, putting on an overflow!

Gentle swells rock, like a lullaby's sway,
As crabs share their dreams of a crumpet buffet.
With shells as confetti, they cheer and they clap,
While unaware sea stars conspicuously nap.

Each splash is a chuckle, each ripple a grin,
Eschewing all worries, letting the fun in.
For in this vast ocean, humor is key,
Reflections of laughter are all that's to see.

Spirits of the Coastal Dreamscape

Seagulls wearing hats, quite the sight,
Chasing soft pretzels, both day and night.
A crab in a tux, he sips iced tea,
Dancing on the sand, wild and free.

A fish with a flair, wearing shades of pink,
Says, "Join me for lunch, let's eat and drink!"
Clams hosting parties, oh what a show,
Laughing and singing, they steal the flow.

The sun's a big joker, it shines so bright,
Splashing all over, a comical sight.
An octopus juggling, how does he do?
Tossing the shells, oh, we're laughing too!

Whales play charades, with a splash and a cheer,
Belly-flops and flip-flops, we all gather near.
The sandcastle crew, their moats are a hit,
While seashells gossip, we can't get enough of it!

A Canvas of Cloud and Waves

The clouds wear mustaches, oh what a sight,
While the sun plays peek-a-boo, day turns to night.
Fish with bow ties swim up to the shore,
Yelling, "What's for dinner? We want a snack more!"

Incredible fluff, the clouds float about,
Puffball pirates shouting with glee, there's no doubt.
An umbrella's blowing, tied to a chair,
It tumbles and giggles, like it hasn't a care!

Kites dance and wiggle, a wild parade,
While turtles tell tales in their sandy glade.
A lizard in glasses reads the day's news,
"It's raining cheerfulness, put on your shoes!"

Pinniped painters, with colors so bright,
Craft murals of fun under the moonlight.
The shore's a big canvas, a joy to behold,
As laughter and colors burst bold and uncontrolled!

Murmurs of the Deep

A dolphin named Dave, with a hat on his head,
Tells jokes to the fish before they're fed.
The seaweed's a dancer, twirls in delight,
As starfish critique the moves late at night.

Turtles tell tales of their journeys afar,
While swimming in circles, they sip from a jar.
A jellyfish joins in with a wiggle and sway,
"Bring on the krill, let's party all day!"

The bubbles are giggling, what a silly sound,
As crabs use their claws to clap all around.
Shells host a concert, with laughter and cheer,
An orchestra of sea-folk, it's their time to steer!

Octopus poets spill ink from their pens,
Crafting a saga of fishy old friends.
Undersea chatter, so funny and deep,
Where joy is contagious, and laughter won't sleep!

Tranquility's Silent Symphony

Breezes whisper secrets, tickling the sand,
While crabs play the maracas, not quite as planned.
A clam taps a beat, with a rhythm divine,
As the cool sea serenades birds on a line.

A seal with a sax, a jazzy charmer,
Starry-eyed fish join in, causing a stir.
Seagulls take center stage, with feathers high,
They strut and they flap, beneath the blue sky.

Splashing and crashing, the ocean's sweet tune,
A dance with the tide, under the light of the moon.
Conch shells are trumpets, playing so bold,
In this tranquil symphony, laughter unfolds.

As laughter echoes softly, the shore calls our name,
Inviting all creatures to join in the game.
With humor and harmony, the sea plays it right,
In a waltz of pure joy, from morning till night!

Ebb and Flow of Bliss

The sea is a jokester, spry and sprightly,
It tosses my hat, making mischief lightly.
I chase those breezes, my hair a wild nest,
But oh, how I laugh, feeling truly blessed.

The seagulls all cackle, with fish in their beaks,
As they swoop down low, playing hide-and-seeks.
I try to throw shells, but they laugh while they fly,
Waving their wings, "You can't catch us, bye!"

The tide pulls my towel, like it's playing tag,
I give it a chase, but it's just a drag.
With laughter we tumble, as footprints we leave,
The beach is a stage, and we're here to believe.

As sun dips below, the sky paints with cheer,
My heart feels so light, it's like flying a deer.
We're dancing with laughter, the moon joins the fun,
In this playful paradise, we frolic till done.

Serene Tides of Dreams

In the calm of the morning, seashells do wink,
As crabs dance in rhythm, not worrying a blink.
They wave their claws high, like they're royalty,
Who knew beach critters could be such a spree?

The sun takes a dip; the clouds wear a grin,
While sunbathers lounge, their sunburns begin.
One ape in a hat, all shades and no care,
Says, "Don't mind the bronze, I'll just glow with flair!"

The kids splash around, like fish out of school,
Pretending to swim in a gigantic old pool.
"Look at me diving!" one shrieks out in glee,
But lands on a jelly and bounces back free!

As the tide rolls in softly, with wishes afloat,
The sandcastles wobble, but still they don't mope.
Laughter surrounds, as the day drifts away,
Each moment of joy, like a game we all play.

Echoes of Coastal Whispers

At dawn, whispers echo, the sea tells a joke,
A donut-shaped wave says, "Hey, give me a poke!"
But I gently retreat, with a grin on my face,
For who knows what tricks it's ready to place?

Sandy toes shuffle, as tide pulls me near,
While a crab in my pocket snickers with cheer.
I insist on a dance; it just crumbles with laughter,
What a delightful disaster, I'm glad I came after!

With sunshine so bright, the shades take a trip,
Gone missing while clowning on my sunbather's lip.
"Bring back those lenses!" I holler with glee,
But a sandcastle knight just stands laughing at me.

As twilight approaches, the critters all sing,
The crickets and gulls make a jubilant ring.
With smiles that sparkle, we toast to the night,
In this land of delight, where the fun takes its flight.

Radiant Currents of Joy

With laughter like bubbles, we float on the foam,
The sea's got a talent, and it feels like home.
A fish jumps in prowess, trying to dance high,
And lands on the pier, as onlookers sigh.

The sun dons its shades, with a wink of delight,
While beachgoers tumble, what a merry sight!
"Come join us!" they call, as I tumble aside,
My belly laughs shaking, just like the tide.

The sandcastles topple, in spite of our care,
While beach bums unite, for a sunburn to share.
"Is that a lobster I see?" one screams in dismay,
But it's only the sunburn, coming out to play!

As dusk drapes its cloak, the laughter won't fade,
We gather 'round bonfires, the night's serenade.
With joy in our hearts, we dance in a ring,
For every bright moment, the next joy will bring.

www.ingramcontent.com/pod-product-compliance
Lightning Source LLC
Chambersburg PA
CBHW072128070526
44585CB00016B/1576